Heartache
and Hope

Heartache and Hope

JILL FLORENCE

Copyright © 2011 by Jill Florence.

Library of Congress Control Number: 2011901092
ISBN: Hardcover   978-1-4568-5704-2
             Softcover   978-1-4568-5703-5
             Ebook   978-1-4568-5705-9

All rights reserved. No part of this book may be reproduced or transmitted in any form or by any means, electronic or mechanical, including photocopying, recording, or by any information storage and retrieval system, without permission in writing from the copyright owner.

This book was printed in the United States of America.

To order additional copies of this book, contact:
Xlibris Corporation
0-800-644-6988
www.xlibrispublishing.co.uk
Orders@xlibrispublishing.co.uk
301408

This book is dedicated to my Grandparents who are no longer with me in this world but who are with me spiritually on a daily basis.

To my Mam, Dad and beautiful Sister who have been there 100% of the time for the boys and me, without them I wouldn't be here.

Contents

Acknowledgments 11
The Peace Lily 13
My Life 14
Wounded, Battered and Bruised. 15
Rush Rush Rush 16
Purple Flowers 17
Confused . . . ??★★★!??? 18
Special Days. 19
Clearing Out. 20
Drowning 22
Salty Water. 23
On the Ceiling 24
Girls, Fun and Lipstick 25
Falling Flesh. 26
Quicksand. 27
Ring Ring. 28
Fat Cats. 29
Shadows and Sunshine. 30
The Frog. 31
The Gates. 32
Answers 33
Turra Show. 34
Small People. 35
Rain~drops. 36
Strategy. 37

The Mask.	38
Ice	39
Seeds	41
Dreams and Hopes	42
Bad . . . . Sad . . . . Glad	43
Sundays	44
The Brief	45
The Invisible String	46
42%	47
Planned . . .	48
Tick Tock	49
Moving On	50
Facebooking	52
Florida	54
Santa's Coming!!	55
Kicking my Heels	56
Stripey Paper	57
Special Friends	58
Undersold	59
One Hundred and Eighty Minutes	60
Who's This?	61
The Truth	62
Eyes of a Wounded Pup	63
The Empty Cup . . .	64
The Car	65
Listen . . .	66
An Angel	67
S.O.S.	68
The Jigsaw	69

Acknowledgments

I would firstly like to thank my wonderful family, especially my Mam and Dad and my beautiful Sister for all the support they have given the boys and me this last two years.

I would never have coped without them, "You are angels and I love you so much." The frantic phone calls and pleas for help were never ignored, they dropped everything to help us. We had some very intense times but they did everything they could to help and still do.

Family are the most important thing in the world and after the heartache that we have been through it affect's the whole family, not just yourself.

I would also like to thank my extended family, you know who you are! for their loyalty to me and the kids and always being there with a hug and a smile even when things are so dark.

My two sweet little boys, for making my life complete! If one good thing came out of this, it is them! They are wonderful little people who when things got tough, every day they managed to make me smile!! Of course not every day was perfect but that's life! They made me see that there was a reason to go on, and even though they are still going through so much pain themselves as they don't see their daddy much, they always ask how I am.

Also I would like to thank my super friends who have listened to me, cuddled me when I needed it, told me to get a grip when I needed it and been there for me whatever . . . you are saints! You really know who your friends are in a crisis and I hope I will be there if any of you ever need me!

Lastly I would like to thank Simone from Xlibris for her support and help in making this happen! She has been so patient and helpful and made it a reality for me. Hopefully this book is closure for me . . . in fact IT IS! x

The Peace Lily.

The peace lily has flowered, it's a sign for me
That we need to change and live in harmony.
We can't go on, tearing each other apart
Let's look at each other and look after our heart.
We'll start from new, with our intended dreams
And keep them up ~ no more screams.
I know what I want, I want to be friends
I love you so much; I don't want this to end.
You're my soul mate, my rock, my pillar, my love
Without you I feel I could never survive.
I give you the chrystal to remember me by
Hold it, get to know it, it may make you cry.
It will help you release emotional stress
It will open your heart and make us hate less.
Carry it with you and give it a feel
I'll do the same and we'll see what's the deal.
Let's get the love back that we no longer see
We can start writing poems, it's about you and me.
We can look at the good things and the things that we'd miss
If we weren't around from hugs to a kiss.
A pat on the bum or a squeeze of the hand
Speaks volumes to me, I don't need a brass band.
We're boy and girl from the very first date
It's a new start this trip, let's wipe that dumb slate.
I love you, I want you, you're all that I need
Without you I'd crumble, I'd be lost indeed.
Let's make that effort, let's push the boat out
We'll be back on track for sure, no doubt.
Happy calls, nice emails will be a good start
Let's get down to basics and open our hearts.

Jf. 30.3.09

My Life.

As I sit and write this poem
I think of what I've done
My life, so precious, so hurt
And sad, and what I have become.
I thought I was the luckiest girl
I had it all and more
My man, my boys, I was content
But now my heart is sore.
Flying high up in the sky
Was how I used to feel
But now I'm down in a deep
Dark hole, and I'm struggling
To keep it real.
The man of my dreams has let
Me down and broken my heart ~
I'm in pain
The thought of living my life
Is hard and won't be the same again.
He's taken my heart, my soul, my pride
And tossed it all away
Selfish, cruel and nasty
Are the words I'd like to say.
But he is weak and I am strong
Good luck is what he'll need
I trust in the great almighty and
He'll suffer for his greed.
What goes round, comes around
He'll remember what he had
Too late mate, you were a great
Amazing, loving dad.

Jf 29.4.09

Wounded, Battered and Bruised.

I'm licking my wounds, I'm battered and bruised
I said "Just come back" he completely refused.
My cuts are deep from my very insides
The pain is intense where love used to reside.
He's cut me in half with a very large knife
He's twisted and turned and ruined my life.
Where love used to flow there's anguish and pain
My mind keeps on thinking again and again.
About what he's done, and all of his lies
Day after day, there's some of us cries.
He's taken away our trust and our pride
Our dreams and our hopes, they've all started to slide.
We're all on our own and it's scary and sad
I ask myself often . . . "was it really that bad?"
But Ian is happy and that's all that matters
Meanwhile were here and our lives are in tatters.
He's taken the core of our family life, and exchanged it
For what? Perhaps a new wife.
It's going to be tough, we're in for a shock
She's got our husband, our daddy, our rock.
The grieving is madness, it's unbearably cruel
All because Ian was a silly old fool.
The 'grass is greener' on the other side
You'll still have the bills, but you've lost your pride.
You're foolish, you're mad, you're clean off your head
Why go there? . . . . be loved here instead.

Jill 9.5.09

Rush Rush Rush....

Rush, rush, rush things to do, it never ends when you're mum and dad too.

Cooking and cleaning, sorting out stuff, spending time with the boys, there's

Never enough............TIME

Time to read, laugh, play games and chill, draw pictures, have capers

When your name is......JILL

Jill, who is she?? What is she?? Does it matter anymore?

She is lost and desperate and needs scraping

From the FLOOR

Floor level is a very good start, this is where I'll start my life

Why am 'I' confused? I knew I was a good WIFE

Wife, yes...what is that? She's the one to care for you in

Sickness and in health. She's the one who put's you first

And love means more than WEALTH.

Jill 11.5.09.

Purple Flowers . . .

I bought a picture yesterday

And it's cheered me up I have to say

It's given me hope and a glimmer of light

For the very first time since that painful night.

I'm doing the walls green

They'll be calming and cool

It may stop me thinking

About that silly old fool.

It's lifted a cloud of grey and black

And made me think "I don't need him back"

The sun will shine on me one day

Inspired by a picture I have to say!!!!

Jill 13.5.09

Confused . . . ??***!???

Confused . . . that's what I am, when I keep thinking
About that silly old bam.
Why did he do this to his family of three?
Maxwell, Jack and oh yes ~ME.
We don't seem important in that man's life
Let's face it . . . I'm only his dumb, stupid wife.
He's so important, so full of himself
He had the lot, happiness and wealth.
But that ain't enough for that stupid old fool
He's goofing around, he thinks that he's cool.
I look at him sadly and remember the days
When we used to be crazy and life was a haze.
Fun and laughter, good crack and love
Being together 24/7 was never enough.
He loved me, adored me, I was simply the best
But hey look what's happened, he's put me to rest.
It's that other woman that has ruined my life
And you know what? I do anything to still be his wife.
I'm hanging on in there, I'm trying so hard
To play this game, when he has the card.
He's the joker, the fool, the full house for sure
But one day he'll realise, that our love was pure.
It's fake, it's not true, what he's up to right now
I hope he'll be happy with that silly old cow.

Jill 29.5.09

Special Days.

Special days are birthdays, they come but once a year
We organise and celebrate, with family that we hold dear.
But this year it is different, the father he has gone
He's left the boys and taken off, it simply is quite wrong.
He seems to think that it's okay, to leave them here
With me, while all the time he's over there
I'm struggling and he is free.
He's cut the ties, he's taken off, he's thrown us all away
He doesn't care, he's happy now, he only has to pay.
Money makes the world go round, it's true it is a fact
But money doesn't make it right, 'cos we had made a pact.
He's broke the trust, he's beared his soul, to the
Devil down below
It makes me sad and worried, 'cos I know where he will go.
He's changed, he's weird, he's gone, completely off
His trolley
I wonder if he really thinks he'll be happy with his dolly??
The master up above, will answer all my prayers
It'll all make sense, I'll see the light, when I
Wander up his stairs.

Jill 2.6.09

Clearing Out.

Boxes, bags and drawers of junk, I don't know what to do?
I've filled up bin bags tied a knot, I've collected quite a few.
My love has gone with a wee holdall, his life is inside that bag
He's left the shirts, the many cards, the ones that said "dear dad"

He doesn't care, he doesn't mind with what he's left behind
Now I'm left here to clear the mess and struggle with what I find.
I've got the marriage certificate, the notes, the cards, the gifts
I don't know what to do with them as they often give me lifts.

I cannot part with our precious past, it's made me who I am
I was a girl, a wife and now I only am a mam.
That small word, it isn't big, but it means a lot to me
For I have something he'll never have, he's blind he cannot see.

My two wee boys, they're six and eight, they 'have' transformed my life
Unlike silly daddy who says, he doesn't want a wife.
I'm making room for all my things, I'm clearing space 'for me'
I find it theraputic and I rub my hands with glee!

It's not, all about him anymore, I'm sick of hearing his name

Who is this man, this loser who is playing this horrid game?

Shiny lights and chests of drawers have appeared at Finnylost

Well what's the point in keeping stuff that previously I tossed.

He's not coming back he's made his point and O~U~T spells OUT

"I'm strong, I'm living, I will survive" is what I'm going to shout.

J.F. 26.5.09

Drowning....

He's at it again,
He's taking me down
I'm gasping for air
I feel I could drown.
Not contented with
Taking my life
He thinks it better
To cause me more strife.
Darker and deeper
I'm starting to slide
All of his promises
He's only just lied.
Why can't he give us
What we truly deserve
He's arrogant, he's stupid
And boy, got some nerve.
I'm worried, I'm weak
I always feel sick
All because of that
Silly old prick.

Jill. 5.6.09

Salty Water.

Salty water trickles down
My face and then my chest
I wipe them hard, I know
This is a very special test.

I don't know why I was chosen
To do this at this time
I think I've been a good girl
I haven't committed the crime.

Tears can make you stronger
They take the dirt away
Time will heal the sore bits
One day, I'll feel ok.

Jf 7.6.09

ON THE CEILING

Tensions high without a doubt,
Stress and lies, I can do without.
Emails, phone calls, make no sense,
When you're wound up, feeling tense.
Scrape me off the ceiling please,
I'm hanging here, but no~one sees
My silent calls, my wishful thoughts,
When it's him that's calling all the shots.
Please help me someone, I'm in despair
I'm floating somewhere in mid~air.
Just take my hand and guide me down
I feel I'm choking, I'm going to drown ~
In all this anger, pain and tears
It's being alone that's what I fear.
I know I'll make it there one day
I'll look around and proudly say
"Hey, look at me and my 2 great boys~
They're my life, my world,
My greatest joys!!"

JF.11.6.09

Girls, Fun and Lipstick . . .

Out tonight to 'my' friend's pad
A virgin vie, it wasn't bad.
Make up, cushion's, bedspread's too
Lipstick's, liner's, there was a few.

Vodka's, vino's, lot's to eat
Sitting laughing, it was a treat.
Us mummy's need to find the time
To chill, relax and feel just fine.

Sharing storie's, sharing shoe's,
Sharing laughter and all the news.
Friend's are special, they are the best
You share with them this 'oddest test'.

'They' put up with all your crap
They're trying hard to fill the gap.
They're doing well, they help
Me through, this awful time
When I feel blue.

j.f.12.6.09

Falling Flesh.

Bones poke through the cotton as I flatten out the seam
The flesh it keeps on falling since this sad and horrid dream.
It is a ghastly nightmare, the one I dreaded most
He promised me that I was safe but he pipped me to the post.
No one can believe that it's him and wasn't me
That did this misdemeanour and spoilt our family.
Up until this last 12 weeks we had a happy time
We laughed, we joked, we did great things
When really all the time.....
He was doing other things which weren't on our list
Secret calls and hidden thoughts
Were all the things I'd missed.
But he was smart, he thought he was so clever and so vain
He was dropping flesh as well, for her ~ it's not the same.
He never cared what I thought about his wobbly tum
I didn't mind the fact, that he had a wrinkly bum.
I loved the imperfections, the bits that weren't right
I didn't mind the fact, that he usually was a sight.
His combat breeks and rough trade top, my god they're still going strong
We joked about the fact that they couldn't last that long.
But he needs them more than he needs me, he's packed them all away
One thing's for sure, I'll never have to see them another day.

JF. 15.6.09.

Quicksand.

Help, I'm sinking in this cold wet stuff
I'm struggling, I'm sinking, I'm running out of puff.
I'm holding out my hand, for a stranger to pull me out
My body's getting smaller, I can hardly even shout.
The life is coming out of me, the spark is fading quick
I need to get some help here please, again I'm feeling sick.
This, quicksand is pulling me down, I'm aching and I'm scared
I'm thinking of all the special times and good things that we shared.
I'm looking back but this must stop
I need to look ahead
If I go on much longer soon
I feel that I'll be dead.
Then he has won and that won't do
I've got to raise the stake
I won't be punished, I won't go down
Because of his mistake.
My neck is almost under, I feel my heart slow down
My eyes are closing, my body aches, because of
That dumb ass clown.
I need a kiss of life, a hand to pull me out
I am a true survivor, I want to scream and shout.
I know that I can do this, I'll quickly raise my head
I'll keep on breathing slowly and remember what he said ~
"Accept it Jill, it's over, I can't change the way I feel"
Well, ok love you've made you're bed,
Now please don't change the deal.
I'm happy to accept, whatever you think's right
But boy if you keep on pushing me
I'll give you the biggest fight
I'm not gone yet, I'm hanging in
I'm weak but I am strong
You'll see in my true colours yet
Believe me it won't be long.

Jf 17.6.09.

Ring Ring

A phone call today—WOW how strange
He couldn't hear, it was "out of range"
Always excuses, always so calm
Never an answer regarding this sham—
Of a marriage that he says, that we had
It didn't seem like it, when he played dad.
Loving and caring, good fun and secure
Reliable, trustworthy, although a tad dour.
These are the things that I miss so much
The hugs and the kisses
The slow gentle touch.
She has it all now, he speaks about "WE"
This is him and her, WHAT—ALREADY???
Why would he speak about them like this?
We don't care about her, it's him that we miss.
Rubbing our faces
In this bucket of myre
Makes me wonder for sure, what will really transpire
About the reasons behind this mess and for why??
It's the answers I need, that may stop me cry.
My hurt and my anger
Are too hard to bear
If only he'd tell me that he did still care.

j.f. 22.6.09

Fat Cats.

11 weeks this has been going on
I wonder why it's taking so long?
All I want is peace of mind
I kinda thought it would all be signed.
He made the deal and I agreed, so what's
The problem? oh yes _ greed.
Fat cat solicitors sitting there
Saying stuff but they don't care.
All they want is their piece of meat
When it's me that's here just wanting to greet.
It never stops it never ends,
This emails and letters that they send.
For what? Oh yes more money of course
They're doing their best but they don't show
No remorse
They're playing with lives and hurting my brain
It's the same old crap over again.
STOP RIGHT NOW and leave me alone
No more letters, I won't answer the phone.
Just sort it out and let me get on with my life
I don't deserve this, I was a good wife.

j.f. 25.6.09

Shadows and Sunshine.

Salty water is drying on my skin, it's hot ~ I'm feeling good
The room is nice, the staff are cool, I'm eating up the food.
3 times a day, it's there, you choose, you don't know what to pick
It's good, I'm feeling better, and hey ~ not feeling sick.
My waist is getting bigger, the choice is quite immense
The tables are so perfect and in a way I sense~
That I must stop thinking, about that man and her
I'm dreaming and I'm wondering and loving how we were.
I feel I have a force here, protecting room 801
It will not settle till it's work in here is sorted and is done.
I sense the shadows, I feel the noise ~ "hello I'm quite aware~
You won't alarm me, or freak me out, it's me ~ you will not scare
I know I'm safe, I have you, it's him that's done the wrong"
I feel like I am sinking so I say "hello, so long"
You got your chance, you don't care now, so what? You Think you're good?
Well get on love 'cos you know what mate ~ you're happy and you should....................
Keep loving baby, it's so damn good, I wish I had the thought
I tried but it's too late now.... boy I really fought.
The sun, it sure don't help, my feelings deep inside
No ~ one's looking at me now I just want to run and hide.
But hey, it's been much better, than sitting still at home
I need to keep on thinking and writing another poem.

Jf.5.7.09

The Frog.

Sweeping up the mess
Outside the playroom door
The dirt, the grit, the papers~
My god and still there's more!
I poked the soft brown mass
Wedged behind the drainpipe
It moved, I squealed oh lord~
I jumped and yes, I got a fright!
The kids they named him 'freddy'
He's now their own pet frog
Well daddy's got a pet now
A great big fluffy dog.
Looking up my book I see
The frog, he means 'detox'
I'll take my sad emotions
And put them in a box.
I need to close the lid now
And put the box away
I'll focus on the good times
That will come to me one day.

Jf. 13.7.09

The Gates.

I'm shattered and sad
He keeps saying it was bad
Don't do this to me
I don't want to be free.
Don't torture me more
'cos I'll land on the floor
I'ts you that's done wrong
Forever how long.
I'm not taking the blame
It was fine till she came
You old fool, you ass
You really surpass~
The last email you sent
I said I was content
I feel sorry for you
You stupid gnu.
An old man, a cheap date
You'll get a rebate
At the gates of hell
You deserve it ~ how swell.

j.f.27.7.

Answers . . . .

A cloud has lifted from the top of my head
My mind is clearer, not wishing I was dead
He phoned tonight for the first time in ages
He said "no arguing please and no more rages"
The emails are filled with such anger from me
But his ones are calm, so how can that be?
I said to him straight that I know what's gone wrong
He listened intently for ever so long.
"Admit it there was nothing wrong with our life,
I did everything right to be a good wife~
But you got your head turned that very first day
Seduced by excitement and the thought of a lay"
His answer was quick and what I wanted to hear
"You're right, 99.9%" God I was near!!
He had convinced himself about all of his lies
Now he'd started on me and to my surprise
I almost believed him 'cos when you're told for so long
You accept what they say even when it is wrong
The feeling I have is of one of relief
I'm still in a state of complete disbelief
I feel I can move on a little today
And maybe tomorrow, there's more that he'll say
To make me feel better from this torture and pain
I want to be happy and feel free again
It's questions I have that I need an answer
Who is she? What is she? A vet or a dancer?
Some people may think that it's not good to know
But for me, it's the only way to get over this blow
That man is the only one who can help me move on
I feel I deserve it, I've waited so long
Come clean, be truthful and please, no more lies
I want to move on and we'll say our goodbyes.

JH 28.7.09

Turra Show

The first Sunday in august is the day of the show
If you fancy a dander and a look you must go.
The smells of the burgers, the gathering crowd
The screams of the kids, my god it's so loud.
You meet lots of people, some known and some not
There's bargains, temptations, there's plenty to be got.
But I don't do that ~ the married boy thing
I know of the dangers, the hurt and the sting.
The pain is intense like a hot burning knife
You never recover ~ it ruins your life.
That's why I'm single, it's bad and it's wrong
I can never work out why it's taken so long.
Why don't men get it, I'm just not that type
It's not that I'm mean but I do have a gripe.
Don't do it, just think, what you're doing is bad
Remember your age, you're not "just a lad"
Respect and some friendship is all that I need
I'm not interested in cheating now that I've been freed.

Jf.3.8.09

Small People.

Don't laugh at me when you're driving me mad

I'm upset and distraught at losing your dad

I know that you're small and you don't understand

Just listen and help me and give me a hand.

I try not to burden you with all of my woes

It's hard for us all and god only knows ~

We're sad and we're angry, we're hurt and we're lost

Our daddy has left us, we treasured him most.

We must stick together and work as a team

I know it is hard and that's how it seems

We will work this out, respect and some thought

Some kindness and help is all that is naught.

I don't want you to worry, I won't let you down

I'm your mam and I love you, I'm not like that clown.

Jf.9.8.09

Rain~drops

Pitter~ patter rain drops

Falling from above

Come and take

My tears away

I'm shedding

For my love.

JF.9.8.09

Strategy.

My friend Karen, phoned me this morning
From Kuala Lumper with a stark warning
"I've seen this before, time after time,
you must stop this crying and draw a line,
Under this mess, you can't change what's happened
I know all your dreams and hopes have been shattered.
Show him you're strong and hold your head high
And whatever you do, try not to cry
Be nice, be happy, pretend you don't care
Let him think you've moved on ~ and don't you dare
Let him see all your pain and anguish inside
Believe in yourself and show him you've tried
To accept what he's done, it's not going to change
I know it's confusing and ever so strange
Let him see what he's missing, you're a wonderful girl"
I'm taking her advice, I'll give it a whirl
I'm changing my strategy, 'cos this one ain't working
He's glad that he's left with all of my sulking
It's justification for leaving us all
From now on I'll pretend that I'm having a ball!!

Jf. 14.8.09

The Mask.

Today my little boy came into my bed
He gave me a cuddle, a smile and said
"I don't like daddy, he's not a nice man"
I held him tight and said "love him ~ you can"
"You know what I think mammy?
Daddy has changed"
I agreed with him completely
It's ever so strange
"he wears a mask, and goes back
To his work, then puts it in his suitcase"
And there it will lurk
He's 6 years old and so on the ball
He can see he's 2 faced
As he had it all
I'm so proud of my boy
He's got him sussed out
The lies and the cheating
We can do without.

J.f 16.8.09.

Ice

He's home today for the next 3 days
"I'm here for an adventure with the boys" he says
He's flippant and arrogant and not very nice
Talking is hard, I can't break the ice

10 minutes of his time is all that I got
I'd get some answers he said ~ I thought
He's not interested in us, we're the bain of his life
His lovely 2 boys and me ~ his wife.

j.f. 20.8.09

In my Head
He is dead
Moving on
He is gone
Ran away
The other day
Haven't heard
Had he cared
He'd be here
Without a fear
He's a sap
He needs a slap
See ya mate
It's way too late
Changed the deal
You are unreal.

j.f. 25.8.09.

Seeds.

'This' week I've felt better
I feel like I've moved on,
He is a distant memory
I think I'm getting strong.
He's made me see that he has
Changed, not for the better either,
At least I see what he's about
And it's given me a breather.
Now sign the deal and leave
Us alone, we'll manage fine I know,
Again it's changed, just keep your cash
And we'll start our lives, we'll grow.
A brand new start, like little seeds
We'll grow against the odds,
The wind, the rain, a battering storm
The great big heavy sods.
We may be weak but soon you'll see
How big we will become.
And one day daddy will be left alone
So lonely, sad and glum.

J.F.29.8.09

Dreams and Hopes.

5 months have passed since this bombshell was dropped
I've struggled, I've wept, I've totally flopped,
This nightmare goes on, it just never ends
The emails, solicitors and rubbish he sends.
I'm sick of his crap and his endless lies, his
Arrogance, obnoxiousness- I totally despise,
I want to move on, I'm thinking ahead, I'm
No longer thinking "I wish I was dead"
I don't want nor need him, he's a waste of
Space
I've got dreams and hopes that I want to chase!
I want to provide for my boys and me
The thought excites me, it's ecstasy!!
New starts and beginnings are what it's about
"We're moving on!!!!......" let's scream and shout!!!!

J.F. 2.9.09

Bad . . . . Sad . . . . Glad.

I've had a lot of better days
Where I think I'm getting by,
I see the rainbow, the shining stars
Way up high in the sky.
It's hard for you to understand
The feelings of disgust,
That I have deep within me,
They're there instead of trust.
Bewilderment and sadness are
The things that drive me mad.
I'm trying 'so' hard every day
But god~it's really hard.
I'm keeping myself busy, I
Did a course this week,
And maybe I will use it
To stop things feeling bleak.
Tonight I made a collage,
Of things that I adore,
I want to do another one
To reach my inner core.
I know that deep within my skin
I've got much more to say,
My necklaces and little words
May change from day to day.

J.F. 17.9.09

Sundays.

Every Sunday is the same
It always makes me sad,
I can't explain the feelings
But they usually are quite bad.
Mondays, Tuesdays, Wednesdays, I
Try to cope quite well,
Thursdays, Fridays, Saturdays
Quite often are real swell.
Then it's Sunday once again
And thoughts come flooding back,
Of how I'll cope and what he's done
And all the things I lack.
I try so hard in all I do, to do
My very best
But this time I failed miserably
I didn't pass the test.
I wasn't quite just good enough to
Keep him here with me
He met and shared with
Another girl and took the opportunity.
It's made me feel a failure, a
Reject and a waste
But that's ok as Ian's good
And he's really got the taste.
Of freedom, no worries, sunny days
My god, it must be great.
He's cleared us from his mind for
Sure, he's really wiped his slate.
It's clean, new starts for him all round
I hope he's feeling proud,
Maybe one day Sundays will be
Fun and really loud.

J.F. 20.9.09

The Brief.

Isn't it amazing, how one can shift the blame,
"it wasn't me" he doth protest, it never stays the same.
It's always someone else's fault, it's defo never him,
The chances that he'll sign the deal
Are really pretty slim.
His empty threats are worthless, I've asked,
He's speaking crap,
She keeps me right, she's very nice and
Never in a flap.
I sometimes wish she'd shout and swear
And tell me he's a 'shit'
But she is a professional,
"we'll wait and get the writ."
I've said I want to keep our home
It's all I've ever wanted,
It's our place, our pad, our sanctuary
I've never taken it for granted.
It's the only thing that keeps us safe
From life's sweet bitter twists,
I'm sick of writing and phoning her
And giving her all my lists.

J.F. 25.9.09

The Invisible String.

Email today ~ he's signed the deal

I'm relieved in a way, but in a way feel

This is the end as husband and wife

I need to start thinking about living my life.

I've got to move on and forget about him

His happiness, his life, it's all just a whim

This is the real life the boys and me do

We're playing it honestly, it's dead, honest true.

The cuddles, the kisses, the sweet gentle tugs

Of the invisible string it's like great big hugs

It'll be with us forever more

My boys who I simply utterly adore.

They are my flesh and blood, they are the best

I feel that we're surviving and passing the test.

J.F. 4.10.09

42%

I'm stuck on 42%, I've been here quite some time
Yesterday was really bad, my head was full of slime.
Mam and dad and sister, were here to pull me through
They've seen me through the bad times,
like when I'm feeling blue.
They've been there through thick and thin,
through happiness and grief
Through joy and laughter, tears and pain,
they've always had belief ~
That I'll get better, that I'll come good,
I'll make it there one day.
That I'll move on and I'll be strong
And I'll turn around and say
"Thank you guys, you are the best
I don't know what I'd do
If you weren't in my family
I've really needed you ~
I'm blessed to have you by my side
As friends may come and go
But you are there forever and I
Hope my feelings show
I love you guys, you are the best
You're always there for me
And one day if you need me back
I'm there eternally"
42% is what I'm going on
Another 58 to go
I'm ready to move along.

J.F. 5.10.09

Planned . . . .

He was a little planner
I didn't really see
Sorting files and cleaning
A busy little bee.
Stashing cash and changing banks
Partly was the plan
I didn't notice, I didn't check
What a greedy little man.
Pretending that his bag was
Full of tins and bags of food
Laughing that he'd packed too much
He'd taken all he could.
He cleared the lot, his paperwork
He'd planned it from the start
I'm struggling still, to still believe
Why he broke my little heart.
Who wants to be with someone
So cruel, so damn right bad?
He used to be so wonderful
Our lovely caring dad.
He's changed so much, he's not the same
She's welcome to his lies
Oh what a shame, it won't be us
It'll be her who sits and cries!!

J.F. 7.10.09

Tick Tock.

The clock's have changed, the time tick's on
I'm feeling still the same
I wish I was a clock myself
And improve my little game.
I feel I'm getting nowhere
Nothing's changed for me
Some day's infact I think I'm worse
I'm lost and jittery.
I feel the panic in my chest
I sometimes slip a pill
When all the time I want to shout
"I'm still the same old Jill!"
I've read back emails from long ago
Where he's said he's sad
And maybe, deep inside me
I'll agree it was occasionally bad.
Maybe we had grown apart
It wasn't quite the same
Although there was some good times
There was always "who's to blame"
Looking back we should've talked
And mentioned how we felt
Instead we just kept going on
Our dreams they began to melt.
It's too late now, I know it is
If I can just hang on
And salvage just his friendship
I know that'll help to keep me strong.
His friendship may be all I'll get
But that will do for me
Then I'll move on and live my life
And quietly let him be.

J. f. 25. 10. 09

Moving On.

The deal's been signed for three weeks now
It's hard to let him go.
I still can't believe what he has done
But my sorrow I cannot show.
"I'm moving on" three little words
They mean a lot to me
I need to turn the corner now
And find my destiny.
I'm doing well, I'm proud of myself
I think I've done not bad
I'm coping fine and most days feel
I'm happy and not too sad.
A nuclear bomb exploded that day
It tore me to the core
A phone call, no answers, it doesn't
Make sense, because of that bloody whore.
The tiny fragments of my life
Still clutter up my mind
I really hoped that I'd be free
Soon after the agreement was signed.
It may take years to get over this
It's hard to say for sure
I'm hoping now that I'm moving on
I'll find a love that's pure.
I'm in no rush, I like being free
With no one asking me why?

*If I go shopping, I see, I want
I take it and I buy.
I'm moving on, I'm clearing out
I'm on the upward trend.
I don't need him, I can do it all
I fix, I treat, I mend
One thing's for sure I know what's right
And who I care for most.
Unlike him and his selfish ways
And all the things he's lost.
My pride, my love, my boys and friends
My home and family
I look and wonder what he's got and
laugh~I'd rather be me!!*

J.f. 30.11.09

Facebooking.

Checking through my face book, thank god I was sitting down
The name, the face, the add~ress, and yes the gloomy frown.

It's him, oh god, I felt sick, but looked, my blood was draining fast
My heart was racing, my face was red, so here he is at last.

I wondered how long it would be before, he paraded his new lifestyle
The flip~flops, the hammock, the beaches and dogs, his girl, it looks worthwhile.

Her name is Ka, not linda, she's dark~skinned with long brown hair
Brazilian no doubt, not american, again more lies, he really doesn't care.

I read the notes and comments "Hey man, you look so happy"
"I love living with you" he said to her, it really is so crappy.

But I'll keep on checking secretly, I'll never let him know
That I know things about him, I've kinda stooped quite low.

I'm sure folk will think I'm foolish, and why do I punish myself more?
I just can't help it, I want to know about him and that stupid whore.

So far I've had no info, and what I got was lies
I never really understood why he had to cut the ties.

But now it's becoming clearer, I'm seeing what's gone on
The pretty girl, the clever one, the sunshine, they have won.

Let's face it, here is boring, it's cold, it's damp and wet
While over there he walks to the beach and already got a sweat.

No kids, no wife, no hassles, his life is free from stress
How great for him, I hope he's proud. For me? ~ I couldn't care less.

         J.F. 23.12.09

Florida

He's coming home, the boys were high, at last, it's been four months
For me it wasn't quite so good, I felt down in the dumps.
The nerves are shattered, the brain is dead, there's nothing more to give
I can't quite grasp the concept that I really need to live.
I got the call, "come to Disneyworld, the boys will have great fun"
I thought a while and checked emails, and thought "let's go to the sun."
'cos daddy's not coming home at all, his visa has ran out
Well there's a thing, If you cared for them, you'd be here without a doubt.
Again another let down, from someone who was good
We can't say that no more for sure, he really is quite rude.
The rides were great, the noise was loud, the entertainment brill
The boys were monkeys most of the time, but all the time I still . . .
Keep thinking hard and working out what really went so wrong
Why the lies and dreadful calls, the cheating going on so long.
I'll never know, he's lied so much, the doesn't know the truth
What bugs me most is his lack of thought, he's totally aloof.
2010 will be a year where I will see the signs
Of all the good things coming to me and all the happy times.
Who wants to be with a grumpy old man? Not me, I want to be free
I'll have some fun and do great things and have some time "for me"

J.F. 23.12.09

Santa's Coming!!

I hear him on the rooftop
He's slipping down the lum
I hear a whimper, a gasp
Of breath ~ he's landed on his bum.

I know he'll fill the stockings
Of all their dreams and wishes
Guitars and drums and a surprise
Or two and maybe even kisses!

They both got clouted on the lips
The blood was everywhere
The screams and shouts and
Streams of blood, I said I didn't care

I did you see but they've been naughty
They had to learn a lesson
It worked a treat, they quietened down
It really was a blessing.

But santa's here and I'm sure
He'll stop, they DO deserve a treat
After what they've been through this year
Is bad, they would like something neat.

The family's altogether, except there's
Someone missing
It will be okay, I'm sure we'll cope
It wont be us he's kissing.
(The boys collided whilst playing, no lasting damage done!)

J.F. 24.12.09

Kicking my Heels.

2000 and 10 has started off well
I'm kicking my heels and feeling just swell
I feel that I'm over that liar and cheat
I've conquered my demons, I think that they're beat
No more energy is being spent on him
I'm sick of the sadness and grieving within
I'm looking ahead and for the first time in ages
I can see that I'm getting there, life without rages
I got some attention one Saturday night
It's hard for me really but it was alright
I'm scared, I feel like a small, tiny kitten
The days are going past and I'm getting more smitten
I'm not ready for love or a big love affair
I just want to be happy, and let down my hair
I'm scared of commitment, I no longer trust
It's friendship and fun that I totally lust
In time I'll get better, I'll let my guard down
It may take some time, because of that clown
I've laughed and I've smiled more this last 5 days
I feel I've escaped from that torturous maze
I'm free, and I'm healthy, I've got all I need
My friend has helped me to plant the seed
One day I'll be bigger and stronger no doubt
You won't take me down, I'm up and I'm out.

J.F. 14.1.10

Stripey Paper.

I'm doing up my bedroom
It's going to be so cool
Stripey paper, chandaliers
No remnants of the fool.
Brand new carpets are coming
Units and mirrors too
A chaise to chill will be just grand,
I'll get a perfect view.
I'm seeing clearer
I'm digging deep into
My very soul
To see what happened, what
Went wrong, and why the big
Black hole.
But I can see that I've made mistakes
It's hard to be so frank
I wish I'd got to rectify
My dreams have all but sank.
I've learnt a lesson the hard way
There's no going back for me
I'm looking forward in many ways
I'm open and I can see.
We had fun, good times and
Laughter and yes there's been some tears
But that's okay let's face it
We'd been US for 22 years.
So open up my bedroom door
I know it will be great
My space, for me, to share and give
For love?? Well that can wait.

j.f. 29.1.10

Special Friends.

Special friends
I have a few
Mainly girls
And some boys too.
They all give
Something different
That satisfies
My needs
I hope that I give
Something back
You don't know
Where it leads.
I don't want
Complications
Some laughter
Some fun
It's time I let
My hair down.
Regrets?
I don't want none.

J. F. 1.2.10

Undersold

Many things have happened since I last put pen to paper
I often thought "I'll do one now" but then may do one later.

Always plenty to be done, the time it passes fast
The ups and downs, the ins and outs, there always is a task.

I started work, I was so chuffed I thought that I was made
I got the call, the desperate shout that I'd been overpaid.

I'm worth the cash I know I am I'm not being undersold
A year is up, I've done the time, I've had my life on hold.

I'm ready now to face the world and show them that I'm strong
I'm confident, and worthy I've feel I've waited so long.

I get an up and then a down and then another up
The strangers home this week I fear I really need some luck.

God give me strength to keep it cool and let him have his say
He doesn't care a damn for us I'll drop my head and pray.

"God keep me safe in your sweet arms and help me understand
why he has changed to a stranger from a wonderful husband."

J.F. 29.3.10

One Hundred and Eighty Minutes.

My poems are wearing thin now
There doesn't seem the need
To write my every feeling and
Fullfill my hungry greed.
The hunger is now passing of
Wanting to make him suffer
I think I'm much more stronger
Now and definitely tougher.
3 hours was all he spent with them
When he came trundling back
Far too busy with his tart
He doesn't have a heart.
One hundred and eighty minutes
Is all they got from him
It's "look at me and my brazilian girl"
And that stupid cheesy grin.
The emails never come now
He doesn't have the time
Rushing round and playing stud
He's just a piece of slime.
We may have turned a corner
We know he won't come back
We got to stick together now
We've given him the sack.

J.F. 4.4.10

Who's This?

Who is the man standing there
A cigarette in hand
I've 3 a day he smugly tells
Back here the fags were banned.

"I don't drink coffee"
He boldly states
I wonder who he is?
Who is this man, this stranger
Who has got me in a tizz.

He never looks me in the eye
He talks so prim and proper
Back then he f'd and blinded sore
About going on the chopper.

He spares no time
He's in a rush, well he is a busy man
"come back tomorrow and see the boys"
"I'll help you if I can!"

He'd things to do and folk
To see, he couldn't spare the time
Showing off his little girl
Was surely the biggest crime.

Her or them? He made the choice
He never saw his other 2 either
It's such a shame he's given up
On his kids for such a diva.

J.F. 15.4.10

The Truth . . . .

I now know the truth, he told me the lies
The desperate pain, the little boys cries
The mother, the anguish, the bleeding inside
The hearts are so broken, they're open and wide

We're trying to mend them but plasters don't heal
The terrible plight and sadness we feel
It's months since he left and still we are torn
The lies and the cheating, and things that he'd sworn

"I'd never do that" are things that he said
When all of the time he was sharing his bed
With a tart off the rig, my god it is sick
It's not company policy to think with your dick.

He promised us he wasn't one of those guys
He's a big fat liar, it was all lies, lies, lies
I now know the truth I'm not really shocked
It's hard to take in as your whole world is rocked

He's a sad little creep who looks like a fool
Fifty three years old, it just isn't cool
Grow up you clown the lies you must stop
I'll never forgive you till the day that I drop

Enjoy what you've got 'cos it's not going to last
Just think of your future and forget your old past.

J.F. 22.9.10

Eyes of a Wounded Pup.

Just when things are feeling good
I go and mess it up,
I just can't cope with jealously and
Eyes of a wounded pup.
He is so right in many ways
He's kind and true and sweet,
But lots of things have changed
For sure and feelings running deep.
I just feel uneasy sharing things,
My life, my boys, my bed,
I think I'm better on my own
"I'm muddled up" I said.
My brain is tired it is a fuzz
It makes me very sad,
That after all this months
Have passed
I still feel really bad.
Please help me god get over this
I cannot clear my brain,
All I want is peace and calm
And free to love again.
18 months on and still it hurts
Like a red, hot burning knife,
Delete my thoughts, my memory
And I'll get on with my life.

J.f. 26.10.10

 Jill Florence

The Empty Cup . . . .

Things have changed for me this week
I'm feeling strong and grounded
The phone call changed things round for me
Not hearing how he sounded.

One kid spoke, the other not,
The first born girl hung up
He doesn't seem to understand
We have an empty cup.

It used to be quite full at times
And sometimes brimming over
The cup of love was there for years
Between two bright young lovers.

I've really nothing nice to say
So I'm better keeping quiet
I'll let the kids all take their turns
Quite soon there will be a riot.

J.F. 31.10.10

The Car

I feel I've turned a corner
It's taken such a time
I'm reaching out for happiness
For something that is mine.
The car has gone, the grey one
I want to brighten up
Anonymous, no that's not me
They'll think I'm lady muck.
I mustn't care, I'll please myself
It's me that matters most
People talk and say bad things
I'm defo not a boast.
"how can she afford it?"
I can hear the whispers now
I'll close my ears and shut my mouth
They'll think I'm a snobby cow.
It makes me feel quite sporty
The shape, the style, the ride
I'm moving on and feeling flash
I don't want to run and hide.
My head is high, I've paid the bill
It makes my head feel clearer
Good thoughts, big smiles and feeling proud
Are things that are becoming nearer!

J.f. 3.11.10

Listen . . . .

He said what he loved was "the old me"
She is the one is wasn't angry
She is the one who had someone to share
The ups and downs, someone to care.

These little people don't listen to me
I threaten, ignore and try to plea
"Please be good and give me respect
I don't ask for much, have you got a defect?"

Maybe it's the ears or some sensory gland
I can shout and yell like a military band
They just turn their ears off and go totally numb
I tell them there's a sweet and then they'll run.

"I'm telling the teacher" has worked well so far
I feel like a failure but I'm stuck in the tar
I need some support and maybe advice
I'm sick of the tantrums, tears and cries.

"We must stick together" are the words that I say
Continually, non~stop, day after day
"Listen for god's sake, just open your ears
Let's smile and be happy, and please no more tears."

J.f. 10.1.11

An Angel.

"A strong man looks after himself,
A stronger man looks after others~
You are a strong woman, 'cos you
Look after us."

These are the words from my boy who is seven
I'm sure he's an angel who was dropped down from heaven
Such words of wisdom from a kid who's so small
He takes it all in and tries to deal with it all.

He struggles to cope with what daddy has done
His mind is a muddle, he think's he's the one
That's done all the wrong and chased him away
It will all become clear, hopefully one day.

J.f. 10.1.11

S.O.S.

A new group has been formed
we're called S.O.S
Survivors of Separation
We're proud and we're blessed
We all have a story
They're often quite sad
But now is the time
To forget about BAD.
It's all about good times
And looking ahead
Forgiving, forgetting
About what's been said
We meet and we chat
And we try to help out
Have speakers, learn new things
Is what it's about.
"Support" and "trust"
Are words that we use
Something we lost
But we're trying to choose
Positive things that
Make us feel great
We're worth it for sure
Let's lighten the weight
Our shoulders can't carry
Much more of the stress
We deserve fun and friendship
And we'll think less and less
About all the past
And what has been done
Reflect and be proud
Of how far we have come. *J.f. 17.1.11*

The Jigsaw.

There are, different people who were put into your life
Some make you happy, some cause you strife
At the end of the day they are there for a reason
Who knows why, some a year, some a season.

One day, they say, it all makes good sense
It's the last bit, of the jigsaw, that makes you so tense
But that is the one bit that makes life complete
It all comes together, we don't have to delete . . . .

The bad things that happen make you stronger inside
You're a fabulous person you don't have to hide
We all learn some lessons, some good and some bad
But that is okay, it is fine to be sad.

Don't be like me and take, too much time
Life is too short to be stuck in the slime
Look forward, be happy, enjoy what you've got
Good health and happiness, it seems quite a lot.

Good family and friends are all that you need
They are the one's who will help you succeed
Embrace what you do have and not what you've lost
We are wonderful people even tho we were tossed.

We hold it together for the sake of the kids
The parent, the helper, the protector of skids
The one who is there at the end of the day
The one who will love you, whatever you say.

J.F. 17.1.11

Lightning Source UK Ltd.
Milton Keynes UK
178664UK00003B/46/P